PENGUINS

MARYSA STORM

BLACK
RABBIT
BOOKS

Bolt Jr. is published by Black Rabbit Books
P.O. Box 3263, Mankato, Minnesota, 56002.
www.blackrabbitbooks.com
Copyright © 2020 Black Rabbit Books

Catherine Cates, designer; Omay Ayres, photo researcher

Names: Storm, Marysa, author.
Title: Penguins / by Marysa Storm.
Description: Mankato, Minnesota : Black Rabbit Books, [2020] | Series: Bolt Jr. Awesome animal lives | Audience: Age 6-8. | Audience: K to Grade 3. | Includes bibliographical references and index.
Identifiers: LCCN 2018053322 (print) | LCCN 2018055074 (ebook) | ISBN 9781623101596 (e-book) | ISBN 9781623101534 (library binding) | ISBN 9781644661031 (paperback)
Subjects: LCSH: Penguins–Juvenile literature.
Classification: LCC QL696.S473 (ebook) | LCC QL696.S473 S768 2020 (print) | DDC 598.47–dc23
LC record available at https://lccn.loc.gov/2018053322

Printed in the United States. 5/19

Image Credits

Alamy: Arco Images GmbH, 5; blickwinkel, Cover; Shutterstock: Alexey Seafarer, 8-9; Christian Musat, 10-11; Christian Rordam, 1; COULANGES, 13; HTN, 22-23; John Yunker, 12-13; Katiekk, 18 (egg, rock); kavram, Cover (bkgd); Kotomiti Okuma, 7; Malykalexa, 6-7 (bkgd); Mikadun, 4; MZPHOTO.CZ, 16-17; Octostockus, 3, 24; Oleh Markov, 14; Robert CHG, 10; Sierra M Clark, 6-7 (penguin); Volodymyr Goinyk, 18; Superstock: Tui De Roy / Minden Pictures, 20-21

Contents

Chapter 1
A Day in the Life 4

Chapter 2
Food and Homes 10

Chapter 3
Family Life 16

More Information 22

A Day in the Life

Penguins leap from the ice. They splash into the sea. Nearby, fish swim. The penguins **glide** toward them. They gobble up the fish. Yum!

glide: to move smoothly

little penguin ⟵ · · · · · · · · · · · · WEIGHT COMPARISON

about 2 pounds
(1 kilogram)

Swimming Birds

Penguins are birds. But they don't fly. Instead, they swim and waddle. Their flippers help them swim.

There are about 17 kinds of penguins. Some are big. Others are small.

▷ emperor penguin
about 88 pounds
(40 kg)

7

Penguin

bill

feathers

flippers

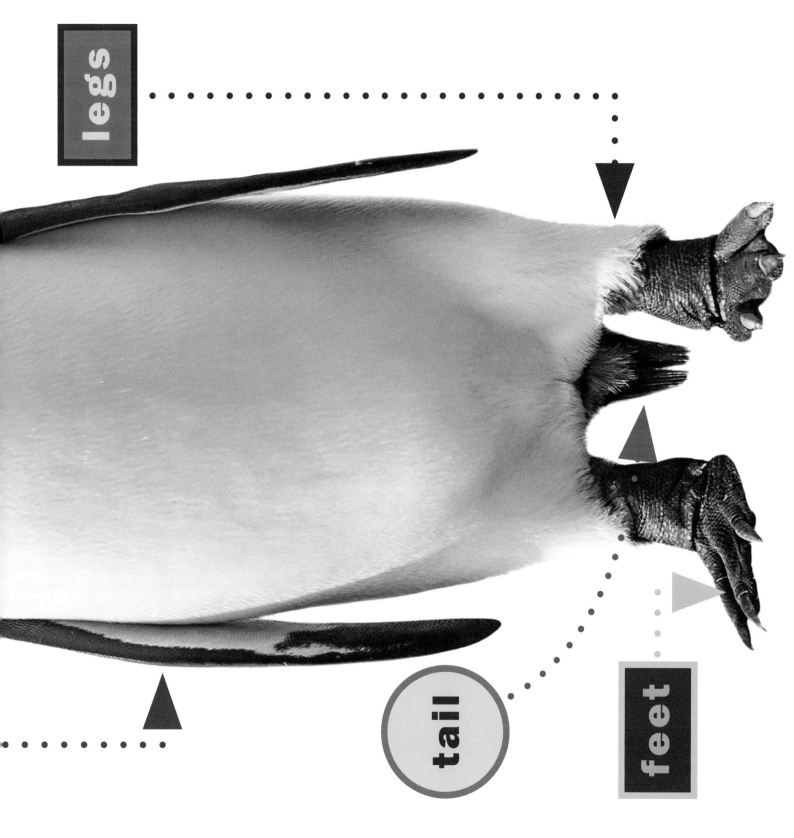

legs

tail

feet

CHAPTER 2

Food and Homes

Penguins eat fish. They also eat **krill** and squid. These birds swim through the water to hunt.

krill: small shellfish

FACT

Penguins swallow their food whole.

Penguin Homes

Penguins live in the Southern **Hemisphere**. They spend most of their lives in the water. Some swim near Antarctica. The water is icy. Their feathers keep them warm. Others live near the **equator**. Their homes are much warmer.

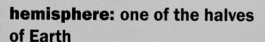

hemisphere: one of the halves of Earth

equator: an imaginary circle around Earth between the North Pole and South Pole

Where Penguins Live

KEY

 = where penguins live

equator

Family Life

Penguins leave the water to have chicks. They gather in groups. The groups are called colonies. Some groups are big. They have thousands of penguins. Others are smaller. They have less than 200.

FACT

Penguins usually gather in the same places each year.

Babies

Penguins lay one or two eggs. After about a month, eggs hatch. Both parents care for chicks. They take turns. One parent watches the chicks. The other hunts. Both hunt when the chicks are older. Growing chicks eat a lot.

Gentoo Penguin Egg's Weight
about .3 pound
(.1 kg)

Bonus Facts

Penguins do not have teeth.

They live 15 to 20 years.

The fastest penguin swims 22 miles (35 kilometers) per hour.

Each chick has its own call.

call: the sound made by an animal

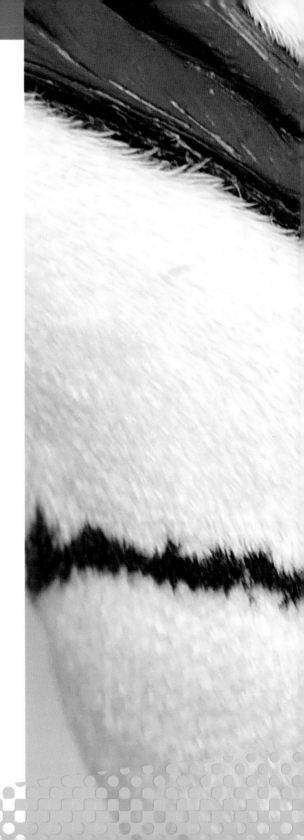

READ MORE/WEBSITES

Gates, Margo. *The Little Penguin.* Let's Look at Animal Habitats. Minneapolis: Lerner Publications, 2020.

Nilsen, Genevieve. *Penguin Chicks.* Polar Babies. Minneapolis: Jump!, Inc., 2020.

Riggs, Kate. *Baby Penguins.* Starting Out. Mankato, MN: Creative Education, 2019.

African Penguin
kids.sandiegozoo.org/animals/african-penguin

Emperor Penguin
kids.nationalgeographic.com/animals/emperor-penguin/#emperor-penguin-group-snow.jpg

GLOSSARY

call (KAWL)—the sound made by an animal

equator (ih-KWEY-ter)—an imaginary circle around Earth between the North Pole and South Pole

glide (GLAHYD)—to move smoothly

krill (KRIL)—small shellfish

hemisphere (HEM-is-feer)—one of the halves of Earth

INDEX

C
chicks, 16, 19, 21

F
features, 7, 8–9, 13, 20
food, 4, 10, 11, 19

H
habitats, 4, 13, 16

L
life spans, 20

R
ranges, 13, 14–15

S
sizes, 6–7, 19